Table of Contents

1. Foreword

2. Disclaimer

3. Introduction: Why Learn About Blockchain and Cryptocurrency?

   - Financial Literacy in the Digital Age

   - Career and Economic Opportunities

   - Understanding the Future of Technology

   - Social and Ethical Awareness

   - Building Critical Thinking Skills

4. Chapter 1: The Basics of Computers

   - What is a Computer?

   - Components of a Computer System

   - How Computers Relate to Blockchain

   - Quiz: Absorbing the Basics

5. Chapter 2: Understanding Blockchain

   - What is Blockchain?

   - Decentralization and Ledgers

   - Nodes in Blockchain Networks

   - Quiz: Blockchain Basics

6. Chapter 3: Cryptocurrency Demystified

   - What is Cryptocurrency?

   - Key Terms: Algorithm, Encryption, Cryptography, Hashing, and Consensus

   - Currency in the Digital World

   - Quiz: Understanding Cryptocurrency Basics

7. Chapter 4: Hashing and Its Role in Blockchain

  - Key Features of Hashing

  - Real-World Analogies for Hashing

  - Importance of Hashing in Blockchain

  - Quiz: Understanding Hashing in Blockchain

8. Chapter 5: Consensus Algorithms

  - Types of Consensus Algorithms

  - How Consensus Algorithms Ensure Security

  - Quiz: Understanding Consensus Algorithms

9. Chapter 6: Bitcoin 101

  - Key Features of Bitcoin

  - How Bitcoin Works

  - Bitcoin Mining Explained

  - Challenges and Opportunities of Bitcoin

  - Quiz: Understanding Bitcoin

10. Chapter 7: Exploring Native Assets in Blockchain

  - Coins vs. Native Tokens

  - Utility Tokens as Native Assets

  - Importance of Native Assets

  - Quiz: Understanding Native Assets in Blockchain

11. Chapter 8: Analyzing Blockchain Projects

  - What is a White Paper?

  - How to Critically Assess a Blockchain Project

  - Red Flags to Watch For

  - Quiz: How to Analyze a Blockchain White Paper

12. Conclusion

- Reflections on the Importance of Blockchain and Cryptocurrency
- Final Thoughts for Readers

Foreword

I am an electrical engineer with a Bachelor of Science from
Northeastern University and an MBA from Suffolk University. At
home I am Dad, and I am known as Uncle Fred. It is 2024 and I am
getting a peek into the future and decided to author this book to help
the young people in my family navigate the recent technology
landscape that is here and forthcoming. Is this an educational book?
Yes. Is this an educational book about making money in the crypto
space, NO! That is for you to discover on your own. Yes, I am an
engineer and yes, I use the term bytes in the title of this book but only
as a fun reference to my computer & engineering friends out there.
Simply put, a byte is a unit of digital information that typically
consists of 8 bits. A bit is the smallest unit of data in computing and
can represent one of two values: 0 or 1, this is the basis of what you
may have heard of as binary code. Don't get nervous!!! I am writing
this to bridge the gap for you. This book will help you understand what
this technology is, how it works, and why it is important to understand.
My goal is to communicate the information in a way that introduces
you to the technical aspects but make it easy to understand. Since
everyone has already heard of it, we are going to start with Bitcoin. As
a point of reference to get started, I asked my 13 And 15-year-old over
dinner, "Hey, have you heard of Bitcoin" They both responded yes,
but when I asked them what it was, one said something people use for
money and the other said it's worth a lot. If that is where you are
perfect, you are in the right place. Are you ready to get started? Let's
go.

Disclaimer

Disclaimer

The information provided in this book is for educational and informational purposes only and should not be considered as financial, investment, or legal advice. The concepts and examples presented are intended to help readers understand blockchain technology and cryptocurrency, but they may not apply to every individual situation. Cryptocurrency and blockchain-related investments involve risks, including potential loss of principal. Readers are encouraged to conduct their own research and consult with a qualified financial advisor, legal professional, or tax expert before making any financial decisions.

The author and publisher assume no responsibility or liability for any financial or investment decisions made based on the content of this book. The views expressed are those of the author and do not necessarily reflect the views of any associated organizations or individuals.

Introduction

INTRODUCTION

Why is it Important to Learn About Blockchain and Cryptocurrency?

As blockchain and cryptocurrency continue to grow in significance, understanding these technologies has become a critical skill for navigating the modern world. Here is why it is important for teenagers and adults to learn about blockchain and cryptocurrency today.

1. Financial Literacy in the Digital Age

Decentralized Finance (DeFi): Blockchain enables decentralized financial systems, allowing individuals to earn, save, and transact without relying on banks. Understanding how DeFi works empowers people to participate in this growing sector.

Investment Opportunities: Cryptocurrencies like Bitcoin and Ethereum are increasingly seen as legitimate investment assets. Knowing how they work helps individuals make informed financial decisions.

Avoiding Scams: Awareness of blockchain technology can help teenagers and adults recognize and avoid scams, such as fraudulent cryptocurrency schemes.

2. Career and Economic Opportunities

Emerging Job Market: Blockchain technology is creating new career paths in fields such as development, cybersecurity, marketing, and data analytics. Learning about blockchain opens doors to high-demand, high-paying jobs.

Entrepreneurship: Blockchain enables individuals to create decentralized apps (dApps), launch tokens, or participate in tokenized crowdfunding, fostering innovation and entrepreneurship.

Global Relevance: As blockchain adoption spreads across industries, understanding its principles will become a competitive advantage in the global economy.

3. Understanding the Future of Technology

Web 3.0: Blockchain is a cornerstone of Web 3.0, the next phase of the internet, where decentralization, privacy, and user control are key. Learning about blockchain helps individuals understand and prepare for this transition.

Tokenized Economy: Assets like art, real estate, and intellectual property are increasingly being tokenized on blockchain. Understanding this process is crucial for participation in modern economies.

Smart Contracts: Blockchain's ability to automate agreements through smart contracts will revolutionize industries, from insurance to supply chain management.

4. Social and Ethical Awareness

Empowerment: Blockchain can provide financial access to unbanked populations and increase transparency in systems like voting and charitable donations. Learning about its potential foster's awareness and advocacy for social good.

Environmental Impact: Understanding blockchain's energy consumption challenges (e.g., mining) encourages young people to innovate and find sustainable solutions.

5. Building Critical Thinking Skills

Complex Problem-Solving: Blockchain technology is inherently complex, requiring individuals to think critically about cryptography, decentralization, and consensus mechanisms.

Digital Responsibility: Learning about blockchain promotes responsible use of digital assets, encouraging people to secure their digital identities and manage their finances wisely.

Chapter 1

Bitcoin, blockchain, crypto currency, is there a difference?

Before you build a house, you must start with its foundation, which is the base structure that provides support for the rest of the house. The foundation of these three terms is computers so let us talk about computers. A computer is an electronic device that processes, stores, and retrieves data. It performs calculations and executes instructions to carry out tasks. Computers consist of hardware (physical components) like keyboard, mouse, hard drive, and software (programs and operating systems) and are used in various fields for tasks ranging from simple computations to complex problem-solving.

The terms blockchain, Bitcoin, and cryptocurrency are often used interchangeably but they are different. Let us get back to foundations, Blockchain is a decentralized and distributed digital ledger technology that records transactions across a network of computers. That was a mouthful, right? Don't worry, I got you. Simply put decentralized describes how blockchain networks control, verify, and stores data. In the field of accounting a ledger is a book or digital record where all financial transactions are systematically recorded and categorized. It serves as the central location for all the accounts of a business. For example, a bank like Bank of America makes use of a traditional network where it has sole control over its ledger. All transactions that happened with the bank and its customers are recorded on the bank's ledger. Therefore, Bank of America is responsible for verifying all the transactions and securing all the data that comes in and goes out of their network. Blockchain networks use a distributed digital ledger which means, there are multiple ledgers, (hundreds to thousands) that are spread across the globe and stored on computer systems called nodes. All nodes are independent. Node owners in a blockchain network are incentivized to ensure the network remains decentralized, secure, and operational. At this point is where I felt that my kids would be at information overload so, here is where I suggest you also pause and go back to re-read this introductory paragraph on block chain to begin shoring up your blockchain foundation.

Quiz: Absorbing the Basics

Section 1: Computers

1. What is the primary function of a computer?

a) To store and retrieve data

b) To perform calculations and execute instructions

c) Both a and b

d) None of the above

2. What are the two main components of a computer system?

a) Keyboard and mouse

b) Software and hardware

c) Hard drive and memory

d) Programs and applications

Section 2: Blockchain Basics

3. What is a blockchain?

a) A cryptocurrency

b) A digital ledger technology

c) A type of computer network

d) A programming language

4. What does "decentralized" mean in the context of blockchain?

a) All control and data are managed by one central authority

b) Control, verification, and storage of data are distributed across a network

c) Data is stored in one central ledger

d) It only applies to cryptocurrencies

5. What is a "ledger" in the field of accounting?

a) A digital system for storing files

b) A record of financial transactions

c) A type of database only banks use

d) A book used for balancing equations

6. How does a traditional bank's ledger differ from a blockchain ledger?

a) A bank's ledger is distributed across multiple locations, while a blockchain ledger is centralized.

b) A bank has sole control over its ledger, while a blockchain ledger is decentralized and distributed.

c) Both systems are decentralized.

d) Both systems rely on nodes to operate.

7. What are "nodes" in a blockchain network?

a) Central servers where blockchain data is stored

b) independent computer systems that store and verify blockchain data

c) Bank employees who oversee blockchain transactions

d) Digital wallets for cryptocurrency

8. Why are node owners incentivized in a blockchain network?

a) To ensure the network remains centralized and controlled

b) To maintain the network's decentralization, security, and operation

c) To keep track of cryptocurrency exchanges

d) To reduce the number of ledgers in the network

Answer Key
Section 1: Computers
c
b
Section 2: Blockchain Basics
3. b
4. b
5. b
6. b
7. b
8. b

Chapter 2

Cryptocurrency

Now let us talk about cryptocurrency. Cryptocurrency, often called "crypto," is a digital or virtual form of money that relies on cryptography for security. Unlike traditional currencies (like the US Dollar or Euro), cryptocurrencies are not issued or regulated by a central authority, such as a government or bank. Instead, they operate on decentralized networks powered by blockchain technology.

Before going any deeper we need to talk about five more computer terms that are important for your understanding because they deal with how data is secured. Algorithm, Encryption, Cryptography, Hashing, and Consensus Algorithms.

An algorithm is a set of clear, step-by-step instructions designed to perform a specific task or solve a particular problem. Think of it as a recipe that guides a process to achieve a desired outcome.

For example:

A cooking recipe is an algorithm for preparing a dish. It includes a sequence of steps, such as gathering ingredients, mixing them in a specific order, and cooking them for a set amount of time.

In computing, an algorithm might involve sorting numbers, finding the shortest route on a map, or encrypting data.

Key Characteristics of an Algorithm

1. Clear and Unambiguous: Each step is precisely defined and leaves no room for interpretation.

2. Input: An algorithm takes some data (input) to process.

3. Output: After processing, it produces a result (output).

4. Finite Steps: An algorithm must have a clear beginning and end.

5. Effectiveness: Each step should be simple enough to be carried out, either by a human or a computer

Encryption

Encryption is the process of converting information or data into a secure code, it is a digital lock-and-key system that takes:

Plaintext: The original, readable data (e.g., a message or file) and creates an Algorithm: which is a set of rules or steps that defines how the data is encrypted (secured) and then the data is locked with an **Encryption Key:** A unique piece of information (like a password) used to encrypt the data. The information is now **Ciphertext:** which is the unreadable, encrypted version of the data.

To access the information, the receiver uses a decryption key to reverse the process. Cryptography is the process of using complex algorithms (cryptography) to secure transactions and control the creation of new coins.

Currency

Let us wrap it up by discussing the currency. Currency is a medium of exchange that people use to trade goods and services. It serves as a standardized form of money, allowing individuals and businesses to assign value to transactions and settle debts. In the United States we use the dollar. In the world of crypto, currency is described by the word coin. A coin is directly tied to and operates as a currency on its own blockchain network. For example, if my daughter Sanaya and son Mason decided to create their own blockchain networks named after themselves, she might call her coin SAN, and he might call his MASE. SAN would be the native asset or coin on the Sanaya network and MASE would be the native asset or coin on the Mason network. This concludes our section on cryptocurrency.

Quiz: Understanding Cryptocurrency Basics

Section 1: Cryptocurrency
1. What is cryptocurrency?

a) A physical form of currency

b) A digital or virtual form of money secured by cryptography

c) A government-issued currency

d) A type of traditional banking system

2. What makes cryptocurrency different from traditional currencies like the US Dollar?

a) It is regulated by central banks

b) It operates on decentralized networks powered by blockchain technology

c) It requires physical coins or bills to function

d) It cannot be used for transactions

Section 2: Algorithms

3. What is an algorithm?

a) A recipe that guides a process to achieve a specific outcome

b) A type of blockchain

c) A financial record of transactions

d) A form of cryptocurrency

4. Which of the following is NOT a key characteristic of an algorithm?

a) Clear and unambiguous steps

b) Produces a result (output) after processing

c) Can have an infinite number of steps

d) Takes input data to process

Section 3: Encryption

5. What does encryption do to data?

a) Deletes the data permanently

b) Converts the data into an unreadable code to secure it

c) Makes the data freely accessible to everyone

d) Organizes the data into a list

6. What is the unreadable version of encrypted data called?

a) Plaintext

b) Ciphertext

c) Algorithm

d) Encryption Key

Section 4: Cryptography

7. What is cryptography used for in cryptocurrency?

a) To physically print coins

b) To secure transactions and control the creation of new coins

c) Managing traditional banking systems

d) To regulate cryptocurrency by governments

Section 5: Currency

8. What is the primary function of currency?

a) To act as a medium of exchange for goods and services

b) To store encrypted data

c) To operate as a decentralized ledger

d) To create new algorithms

9. What is a coin in cryptocurrency?

a) A physical representation of crypto

b) A digital asset tied directly to its own blockchain network

c) A software program used in blockchain

d) A tool for encrypting data

10. If Mason and Sanaya created their own blockchain networks, what would their native coins be called?

a) Mason and Sanaya

b) Blockchain Dollars

c) SAN and MASE

d) USD and Crypto

Answer Key
1. b
2. b
3. a
4. c
5. b
6. b
7. b
8. a
9. b
10. c

Chapter 3

Hashing

What is Hashing in Blockchain? Hashing in blockchain is the process of converting input data (of any size) into a fixed-length, unique string of characters, called hash, using a mathematical algorithm. Hashing is fundamental to blockchain technology because it ensures the integrity, security, and immutability of the data stored on the blockchain.

Key Features of Hashing

1. Fixed-Length Output:

Regardless of the size of the input data, the hash output is always a fixed length.

Example: A 100-word document and a single word will produce hashes of the same length.

Popular Algorithm Example: SHA-256 produces 256-bit hash.

2. Deterministic:

The same input will always generate the same hash output.

3. Irreversible:

It is computationally infeasible to determine the original input from the hash output.

4. Unique Output:

Even an insignificant change in the input data will produce an entirely different hash, a property known as the Avalanche Effect.

5. Efficient:

Hashing algorithms can process data quickly, making them suitable for large datasets.

How Hashing Works in Blockchain

1. Data Integrity:

Every block in a blockchain contains a hash of its data. If even a single piece of data in the block is altered, the hash changes, signaling tampering.

2. Linking Blocks:

Each block contains the hash of the previous block, forming a chain. This ensures that altering one block would require altering all subsequent blocks, which is nearly impossible.

3. Mining:

In Proof of Work (PoW) systems, miners solve a computational puzzle by finding a hash that meets specific criteria (e.g., a certain number of leading zeroes). This is called nonce discovery.

4. Digital Signatures:

Hashing ensures that transactions in the blockchain are secure and unaltered during transmission.

Examples of Hashing

- Using the SHA-256 algorithm:
- Input 1: Hello, Blockchain!
- Hash 1:
  5c53c6cf0caff5d55d1163b62714b89f37d1f3fa7c3d892f2e9e1eec8a1
  0d8d6

- Input 2: Hello, Blockchain.
- **(Note the period instead of exclamation mark)**
- Hash 2:
  b315aa7e554ba408e8f6b8af4bc1cbf3e1e765db0ac80ef19f21382d71
  d7e009. Even a small change in the input creates a completely
  different hash.

Why is Hashing Important in Blockchain?

1. Data Security:

Hashing ensures that data stored on the blockchain cannot be altered without detection.

2. Immutability:

By linking blocks with hashes, the blockchain creates a tamper-proof ledger.

3. Efficiency:

Hashing enables quick verification of data, which is essential for blockchain's decentralized operations.

Real-World Analogy

Imagine a document being run through a paper shredder, producing a pile of confetti. The pile represents the hash—unique to that document. While you can easily shred the same document again and get the same pile, it is nearly impossible to reconstruct the original document from the shredded pieces.

Quiz: Understanding Hashing in Blockchain

Section 1: Basics of Hashing

1. What is hashing in blockchain?

a) Encrypting data to keep it secure

b) Converting input data into a fixed-length unique string using a mathematical algorithm

c) Storing data in blocks for easy retrieval

d) Compressing data to save storage space

2. What is the output of a hashing algorithm called?

a) Ciphertext

b) Digital key

c) Hash

d) Block

3. Which of the following is true about a hash?

a) It is always the same length, regardless of the input size

b) It is reversible with the right algorithm

c) It changes randomly for the same input data

d) It can store multiple data points

Section 2: Properties of Hashing

4. What happens if you change even one character in the input data?

a) The hash output remains the same

b) The hash output changes completely

c) The hash output becomes twice as long

d) The input cannot be hashed again

5. Which property of hashing makes it impossible to determine the original input from the hash?

a) Deterministic nature

b) Irreversibility

c) Fixed-length output

d) Avalanche Effect

6. What is the Avalanche Effect in hashing?

a) The process of linking blocks in a blockchain

b) A property where even a tiny change in input causes a completely different hash

c) The collapse of a blockchain network due to too many blocks

d) The increase in hash size when input data grows

Section 3: Hashing in Blockchain

7. How does hashing contribute to the security of blockchain?

a) By encrypting transactions before they are broadcast

b) By linking blocks together with unique hashes

c) By reversing hashed data for validation

d) By compressing transaction data into smaller blocks

8. What role does hashing play in blockchain mining?

a) Miners must solve a specific hash to validate a block

b) Hashing is used to encrypt mined Bitcoin

c) Hashes determine how many coins a miner can earn

d) Hashing compresses the mining rewards into smaller amounts

9. Which hashing algorithm is commonly used in Bitcoin mining?

a) SHA-256

b) AES-128

c) RSA

d) MD5

10. What happens if a block's hash is altered in a blockchain?

a) It causes all subsequent blocks' hashes to change

b) The block is automatically deleted

c) The blockchain ignores the change and continues

d) The blockchain recreates the hash to match the data

Answer Key
Section 1: Basics of Hashing
b | 2. c | 3. a
Section 2: Properties of Hashing
4. b | 5. b | 6. b
Section 3: Hashing in Blockchain
7. b | 8. a | 9. a | 10. a

Chapter 4

What Are Consensus Algorithms in Blockchain?

A consensus algorithm is a mechanism used in blockchain networks to ensure that all participants (nodes) agree on the state of the blockchain. It is essential for maintaining the integrity, security, and decentralized nature of the blockchain by validating transactions and adding new blocks to the chain.

Why Are Consensus Algorithms Important?

In a decentralized network, where there is no central authority, consensus algorithms:

1. Ensure Trust: Enable participants to trust the system without needing to trust each other directly.

2. Validate Transactions: Confirm that only legitimate transactions are added to the blockchain.

3. Maintain Security: Prevent malicious actors from tampering with the blockchain or creating false data.

4. Enable Decentralization: Allow the network to operate collectively without a central control point.

Types of Consensus Algorithms

Here are some of the most common consensus algorithms used in blockchain:

1. Proof of Work (PoW): Works using Nodes (miners) that compete to solve complex mathematical puzzles. The first to solve it validates the block and adds it to the blockchain. This consensus algorithm is used by: Bitcoin, & Litecoin.

Pros:

- Highly secure.
- Resistant to tampering.

Cons:

- Energy-intensive.
- Slower transaction speeds

2. Proof of Stake (PoS): Works by choosing validators to create new blocks based on the amount of cryptocurrency they hold and are willing to "stake" as collateral. This consensus algorithm is used by: Ethereum (since Ethereum 2.0), Cardano, Solana.

Pros:

- Energy-efficient.
- Encourages long-term commitment.

Cons:

- Wealth concentration risk (those with more stake have more influence).

3. Delegated Proof of Stake (DPoS): this works by participants voting to elect a small group of validators to secure the blockchain on their behalf. This consensus algorithm is used by EOS, TRON.

Pros:

- Faster transactions.
- Lower energy consumption

Cons:

- Centralization risk (power concentrated among elected validators).

4. Proof of Authority (PoA): works by using pre-approved and known validators making it suitable for private or permissioned blockchains. This consensus algorithm is used by: VeChain, some private Ethereum networks.

Pros:

- Extremely fast.
- Low energy usage.

Cons:

- Not fully decentralized.

5. Proof of Burn (PoB): This works by participants "burn" (destroying) a portion of their cryptocurrency to gain the right to validate transactions and create new blocks. This consensus algorithm is used by: Slimcoin.

Pros:

- Discourages spam and malicious behavior.

Cons:

- Wasteful as it involves destroying value.

6. Proof of History (PoH): This works using a cryptographic clock to timestamp transactions to prove that they occurred in a specific order, enabling faster consensus. This consensus algorithm is used by: Solana (in conjunction with PoS).

Pros:

- Extremely fast.
- Ideal for high-throughput networks.

Cons:

- Requires sophisticated implementation.

How Consensus Algorithms Ensure Security

1. Tamper Resistance: If a block is altered, the consensus algorithm detects inconsistency, preventing fraud.

2. Fault Tolerance: Consensus mechanisms allow the blockchain to function even if some nodes are unreliable or malicious (e.g., Byzantine Fault Tolerance).

3. Decentralized Control: Consensus spreads decision-making across the network, preventing centralized control.

Real-World Analogy

Imagine a group of people trying to decide on where to have lunch. Without a leader, they all vote (or come to consensus) on the best option. Similarly, consensus algorithms help blockchain participants collectively agree on which transactions are valid and should be added to the chain.

Quiz: Understanding Consensus Algorithms

Section 1: Basics of Consensus
1. What is a consensus algorithm in blockchain?

a) A process used to create new cryptocurrencies

b) A mechanism to ensure all participants agree on the state of the blockchain

c) A tool for encrypting transactions

d) A centralized system for controlling the blockchain

2. Why are consensus algorithms important?

a) They allow central authorities to manage the blockchain

b) They validate transactions and maintain the blockchain's security

c) They prevent blockchains from being decentralized

d) They increase the transaction fees on the network

Section 2: Types of Consensus Algorithms

3. Which consensus algorithm does Bitcoin use?

a) Proof of Stake (PoS)

b) Proof of Work (PoW)

c) Delegated Proof of Stake (DPoS)

d) Proof of Authority (PoA)

4. What is a key disadvantage of Proof of Work (PoW)?

a) It is energy-intensive

b) It is slower than other algorithms

c) It requires high transaction fees

d) Both a and b

5. How does Proof of Stake (PoS) choose validators?

a) Based on the amount of cryptocurrency they hold and stake

b) By solving complex mathematical puzzles

c) By voting for elected representatives

d) By destroying a portion of their cryptocurrency

6. Which consensus algorithm allows participants to vote for validators?

a) Proof of Work (PoW)

b) Proof of Stake (PoS)

c) Delegated Proof of Stake (DPoS)

d) Proof of History (PoH)

Section 3: Advanced Concepts

7. What is the main advantage of Proof of Authority (PoA)?

a) It is highly decentralized

b) It is extremely fast and energy-efficient

c) It does not require validators

d) It uses high levels of cryptography

8. Which blockchain uses Proof of History (PoH) for faster transaction validation?

a) Bitcoin

b) Ethereum

c) Solana

d) Cardano

9. What is Byzantine Fault Tolerance (BFT)?

a) A feature of blockchains that prevents double-spending

b) The ability of a blockchain to function despite unreliable or malicious nodes

c) A type of encryption used for transaction validation

d) A voting mechanism for electing miners

10. What happens during a Bitcoin mining process under Proof of Work?

a) Validators are selected based on their stake

b) Nodes solve complex puzzles to validate transactions

c) Coins are burned to secure the network

d) A group of validators votes on the next block

Answer Key
Section 1: Basics of Consensus
b | 2. b
Section 2: Types of Consensus Algorithms
3. b | 4. d | 5. a | 6. c
Section 3: Advanced Concepts
7. b | 8. c | 9. b | 10. b

Chapter 5

Bitcoin

Now that we have the foundations let us talk Bitcoin. Bitcoin is the first and most well-known cryptocurrency, introduced in 2009 by an anonymous person or group of people using the pseudonym Satoshi Nakamoto. It is a decentralized digital currency that allows people to send and receive payments over the internet without the need for intermediaries, like banks or payment processors. There are five key features that created Bitcoin's claim to fame. It's decentralized, can be used for Peer-to-Peer Transactions: Bitcoin enables direct transactions between users without requiring a middleman. For example, you can send Bitcoin to a friend anywhere in the world, and the transaction will be verified by the network. It is of limited supply: There will only ever be twenty-one million Bitcoins in existence. This limited supply makes Bitcoin scarce, similar to gold, and has contributed to its value as a digital asset. Bitcoin is secure by design: Bitcoin uses blockchain technology to maintain a transparent, tamper-proof ledger of all transactions. The network is secured by advanced cryptographic techniques, making it highly resistant to hacking or fraud. Last, it is global and borderless: Bitcoin transactions can be made across the globe without being affected by exchange rates, banking hours, or political boundaries.

How Does Bitcoin Work?

Bitcoin relies on blockchain technology to function. Here is a simplified breakdown:

1. Digital Wallets: To use Bitcoin, you need a digital wallet. A wallet has a public key (similar to an account number) and a private key (like a password) to send and receive Bitcoin.

2. Transactions: When you send Bitcoin, the network verifies the transaction using a process called mining. Once verified, the transaction is added to the blockchain.

3. Blockchain: The blockchain is a public ledger that records all Bitcoin transactions. It ensures transparency and prevents double-spending (the same Bitcoin being used in multiple transactions).

What is Bitcoin Used For?

1. Digital Payments: Bitcoin can be used to purchase goods and services from merchants and online platforms that accept it.

2. Investment: Many people view Bitcoin as "digital gold" and invest in it as a store of value or hedge against inflation.

3. Remittances: Bitcoin allows for quick, low-cost international money transfers compared to traditional methods.

4. Decentralized Applications: Bitcoin inspires and supports the development of decentralized technologies.

Challenges of Bitcoin

1. Volatility: Bitcoin's price can fluctuate significantly, which can make it risky for investors or impractical for everyday transactions.
2. Scalability: The network can process a limited number of transactions per second, which can lead to delays during periods of high demand.
3. Energy Consumption: Bitcoin mining requires a large amount of computational power, raising concerns about its environmental impact.

Bitcoin Mining: The Heart of the Network

Bitcoin mining is a critical process that keeps the Bitcoin network secure and operational. It is the method through which new Bitcoins are created, and transactions are verified on the blockchain. Let us break it down:

What is Bitcoin Mining? Bitcoin mining is the process of solving complex mathematical problems using powerful computers to:

1. Verify Transactions: Ensuring all Bitcoin transactions are valid and not fraudulent.
2. To add Blocks to the Blockchain: Once verified, transactions are grouped into a block and added to the blockchain.
3. Create New Bitcoins: As a reward for their work, miners receive newly minted Bitcoins.

Think of mining as a global competition where miners race to solve a puzzle. The winner gets to:

Add the next block of transactions to the blockchain.

Earn a reward in Bitcoin (currently 6.25 BTC per block, but this amount halves roughly every four years in an event called the halving).

How Does Mining Work? Here is a simplified analogy, imagine a large group of people trying to guess the combination of a safe that contains a prize. Each person (miner) makes random guesses until someone gets it right. Once the combination is cracked:

1. The winner opens the safe (solves the puzzle).

2. They take the prize (the Bitcoin reward).

3. The process resets, and everyone starts guessing the next combination.

In Bitcoin mining:

The Safe: The mathematical problem that miners need to solve.

The Prize: New Bitcoins and transaction fees from the block.

The Guessing: Miners use computational power to try millions of solutions per second.

This process uses a mechanism called Proof of Work (PoW) to secure the blockchain.

Why is Mining Important?

1. Security: Mining ensures that transactions are valid, and the network is tamper-proof.

2. Decentralization: Mining is done by individuals and organizations worldwide, keeping the network free from central control.

3. Bitcoin Creation: Mining is the only way new Bitcoins are introduced into circulation.

Challenges of Mining

1. Energy Consumption: Mining requires a significant amount of electricity to power the hardware, raising concerns about its environmental impact.

2. Competition: Mining has become highly competitive, requiring expensive equipment and significant resources to be profitable.

3. Difficulty Adjustments: The Bitcoin network adjusts the difficulty of the puzzles every two weeks to maintain a steady flow of new blocks (about one block every 10 minutes).

Real-World Analogy for Bitcoin Mining

Think of Bitcoin mining as a global treasure hunt. Miners are like adventurers solving riddles to find hidden treasure. Each riddle gets harder over time, but the reward remains valuable. The blockchain is the treasure map, and every successful riddle adds a new path to the map, visible to everyone.

Projected Timeline for Mining All Bitcoin

The last Bitcoin is expected to be mined around the year 2140. This is because the halving process slows down the rate at which new Bitcoin is created, making it take longer to mine the remaining supply over time. By 2140, miners will no longer receive new Bitcoin as a reward but will earn income from transaction fees as incentives to maintain the network.

What is Scarcity?

Scarcity refers to the limited availability of a resource in contrast to the demand for it. When something is scarce, its value tends to increase if there is significant demand for it.

Scarcity and Bitcoin

Limited In Supply: With only twenty-one million Bitcoin ever available, the supply is fixed and cannot be increased. Growing Demand: As more people, businesses, and institutions adopt Bitcoin, its demand increases. Since no new supply can be created beyond the cap, scarcity drives up its value.

How Scarcity Adds Value to Bitcoin

1. Finite Supply: Unlike fiat currencies, which can be printed endlessly by central banks, Bitcoin's supply is mathematically limited, making it predictable and resistant to inflation.

2. Comparison to Gold: Bitcoin is often referred to as "digital gold" because it shares similar characteristics: Both are scarce. Both require effort to "mine" (gold from the earth, Bitcoin from solving cryptographic problems). Both are considered a store of value.

3. Investor Confidence: Scarcity creates a perception of value. Investors see Bitcoin as a deflationary asset, meaning its purchasing power is expected to increase over time as demand rises.

4. Network Effect: The more people adopt Bitcoin, the greater its utility and perceived value, amplifying the effects of scarcity.

Real-World Example of Scarcity and Value
Consider a rare collectible, like a limited-edition sports card or a rare painting. If there are only twenty-one cards or paintings in the world, and demand grows over time, their value will likely increase because they cannot be reproduced. Bitcoin operates similarly, but on a global and digital scale.

Quiz: Understanding Bitcoin

Section 1: Bitcoin Basics

1. What is Bitcoin?

a) A government-regulated digital currency

b) The first decentralized cryptocurrency

c) A payment system controlled by banks

d) A physical form of cryptocurrency

2. Who created Bitcoin?

a) Elon Musk

b) Vitalik Buterin

c) Satoshi Nakamoto

d) Tim Berners-Lee

3. How many Bitcoins will ever exist?

a) 50 million

b) 1 billion

c) 21 million

d) Unlimited

4. What is the main purpose of Bitcoin's blockchain?

a) To print physical coins

b) To record and verify transactions in a secure, decentralized way

c) To manage a central bank's database

d) To create infinite digital assets

Section 2: Bitcoin Mining

5. What is Bitcoin mining?

a) Extracting digital currency from physical mines

b) Using computers to solve mathematical problems and verify transactions

c) A process controlled by banks to create Bitcoin

d) Printing Bitcoin onto digital wallets

6. What happens during a Bitcoin halving event?

a) The supply of Bitcoin doubles

b) Mining rewards are reduced by half

c) The number of miners decreases by half

d) All transactions are erased from the blockchain

7. When is the last Bitcoin expected to be mined?

a) 2040

b) 2140

c) 2025

d) 2035

Section 3: Scarcity and Value

8. Why is Bitcoin considered scarce?

a) It is a natural resource like gold

b) Its supply is limited to 21 million coins

c) Governments control how much Bitcoin can be mined

d) Only a few people know how to create Bitcoin

9. What is one reason scarcity adds value to Bitcoin?

a) The blockchain can create new coins indefinitely

b) Scarcity reduces its volatility

c) Fixed supply and growing demand increase its perceived value

d) Bitcoin is controlled by central banks

10. Why is Bitcoin compared to gold?

a) Both are mined and have limited supply

b) Both are physical assets

c) Both can be easily printed

d) Both are regulated by governments

Answer Key
Section 1: Bitcoin Basics
b | 2. c | 3. c | 4. b
Section 2: Bitcoin Mining
5. b | 6. b | 7. b
Section 3: Scarcity and Value
8. b | 9. c | 10. a

Chapter 6

Are Coins the Only Native Assets in Blockchain?

No, coins are not the only native assets in blockchain networks. While coins like Bitcoin (BTC) and Ether (ETH) are among the most well-known native assets, other forms of native assets exist, depending on the purpose and design of the blockchain.

Types of Native Assets in Blockchain

1. Coins

A coin is a cryptocurrency that operates as the primary currency of its blockchain.

Examples:

- **Bitcoin (BTC):** The native asset of the Bitcoin blockchain.
- **Ether (ETH):** The native asset of the Ethereum blockchain.

Purpose: Coins are typically used for transactions, as a store of value, or to pay for services on the blockchain.

2. Native Tokens

Some blockchains have native tokens that represent a unit of value within their ecosystems, but they serve purposes beyond being a currency.

Examples:

- **XRP:** The native token of the Ripple network, used for facilitating cross-border payments.
- **DOT:** The native token of the Polkadot blockchain, used for governance and staking.

Purpose: Native tokens often have specialized roles, such as: Enabling governance (voting on network changes). Staking to secure the network. Paying transaction fees.

3. Utility Tokens as Native Assets

Some blockchains are designed around specific applications, and their native assets function as utility tokens within that ecosystem.

Examples:

- **FIL:** The native token of the Filecoin network, used for storage and retrieval services.
- **GRT:** The native token of The Graph, used to query and index data on blockchains.

Purpose: These native tokens power the blockchain's unique service.

Why Are Native Assets Important?

1. Ecosystem Functionality: Native assets provide the necessary incentives and tools for blockchains to operate effectively. For example: coins are used to pay transaction fees or rewards to miners. Tokens enable specialized features like governance or staking.

2. Decentralization: Native assets ensure that no single entity controls the blockchain, as they distribute power among participants.

3. Incentives: They motivate users and validators to participate in the network by offering rewards or staking opportunities.

While coins like Bitcoin and Ether are the most recognized native assets, native tokens and utility tokens also play critical roles in their respective blockchain ecosystems. These assets expand the possibilities of blockchain technology beyond digital currency, enabling governance, utility services, and specialized applications.

Quiz: Understanding Native Assets in Blockchain

Section 1: Basics of Native Assets

1. What is a native asset in blockchain?

a) A digital currency created by users

b) An asset directly tied to and operating on its own blockchain

c) A token used for governance on any blockchain

d) A physical representation of cryptocurrency

2. What is the primary purpose of native assets?

a) To act as a currency or provide functionality within a blockchain ecosystem

b) To replace fiat currency entirely

c) To provide physical tokens for users

d) To store transaction data offline

3. Which of the following is an example of a coin as a native asset?

a) XRP

b) FIL

c) BTC

d) USDT

Section 2: Coins vs. Native Tokens

4. What is the difference between coins and native tokens?

a) Coins operate on their own blockchain, while native tokens are tied to existing ecosystems

b) Coins can only be used for transactions, while tokens cannot

c) Coins are centralized, while tokens are always decentralized

d) Coins have unlimited supply, while tokens are finite

5. Which of the following is an example of a native token?

a) ETH

b) DOT

c) BTC

d) ADA

6. What is a common use of native tokens in blockchain ecosystems?

a) Paying transaction fees

b) Facilitating governance through voting

c) Staking to secure the network

d) All of the above

Section 3: Utility of Native Assets

7. What type of native asset powers the Filecoin network?

a) FIL

b) XRP

c) DOT

d) BTC

8. Which blockchain uses XRP as its native token for cross-border payments?

a) Ethereum

b) Ripple

c) Solana

d) Polkadot

Section 4: Advanced Concepts

9. How do native tokens often differ from coins in their blockchain ecosystems?

a) Tokens focus on providing specific utilities beyond being a medium of exchange

b) Tokens are exclusively used in private blockchains

c) Tokens are always controlled by a central authority

d) Tokens cannot be used for staking or governance

10. Why are native assets important to blockchain ecosystems?

a) They incentivize participation and secure the network

b) They create infinite supply for users

c) They allow only centralized control of the blockchain

d) They remove the need for blockchain governance

Answer Key
Section 1: Basics of Native Assets
b | 2. a | 3. c
Section 2: Coins vs. Native Tokens
4. a | 5. b | 6. d
Section 3: Utility of Native Assets
7. a | 8. b
Section 4: Advanced Concepts
9. a | 10. a

Chapter 7

What is White Paper in Blockchain?

As mentioned in the beginning of the text, this book isn't to teach you how to invest in cryptocurrencies or financial advice. If you've made it this far it's because there is an interest in the technology and are seeking more information. If you're interested in a specific blockchain project, or cryptocurrency, the most important thing you can do is read its White Paper. A white paper in the context of blockchain is an official document that provides detailed information about a blockchain project or cryptocurrency. It serves as a comprehensive guide that explains the project's purpose, technology, use cases, and goals to potential investors, developers, and users.

Key Features of a Blockchain White Paper

1. Project Overview:

- Describes the problem the project aims to solve.
- Explains how the project plans to address the problem using blockchain technology.

2. Technical Details:

- Provides a deep dive into the technology behind the project, such as the blockchain architecture, consensus algorithm, and cryptographic methods used.
- Outlines how the system operates, including transaction mechanisms and security measures.

3. Tokenomics:

- Details the role of the native token (if applicable), including its supply, distribution, and use cases within the ecosystem.
- Explains how users, developers, or miners are incentivized.

4. Roadmap:

- Lays out the timeline for project milestones and future developments.
- Includes planned updates, new features, or expansions.

5. Team Information:

- Introduces the core team members, advisors, and developers behind the project.
- Builds trust and credibility with investors and the community.

6. Call to Action:

- Provides information about how to participate in the project, such as through an Initial Coin Offering (ICO), staking, or using the platform.

Uses of a Blockchain White Paper

1. Educating Stakeholders:

- Provides clear, detailed information for potential investors, developers, and users to understand the project.

2. Building Credibility:

A well-written white paper shows that the project has been thoroughly planned, which helps attract investment and build trust within the blockchain community.

3. Attracting Investment:

- Many blockchain projects use white papers as a key tool during fundraising events like ICOs, where they explain the value and utility of their token.

4. Setting Expectations:

- The white paper acts as a blueprint for the project's future, outlining milestones and goals.

5. Guiding Development:

- It serves as a reference document for the development team, ensuring everyone is aligned with the project's vision.

Example of a Famous Blockchain White Paper

Bitcoin White Paper (2008): Written by Satoshi Nakamoto, it introduced Bitcoin as "a peer-to-peer electronic cash system." It detailed how Bitcoin's blockchain would use Proof of Work for consensus, eliminate intermediaries, and solve the double-spending problem.

Importance of Reading a White Paper

For potential investors or users, reading a white paper is crucial because it:

- Helps identify whether the project has real-world value or is just hype.
- Reveals the level of expertise and planning behind the project.
- Explains the potential risks, rewards, and functionality of the technology.

How to Analyze a Blockchain White Paper

When analyzing a blockchain white paper, the goal is to evaluate its credibility, feasibility, and potential value. Below is a step-by-step guide to help you critically assess the document:

1. Understand the Project's Vision

Key Questions:

- What problem does the project aim to solve?
- Is the problem significant and relevant in the real world?
- Does the blockchain solution make sense for this problem, or is it unnecessary hype?

Tip: Look for a clear and concise explanation of the project's purpose. If the goals seem vague or overly ambitious, proceed cautiously.

2. Evaluate the Use of Blockchain Technology

Key Questions:

- Why does this project need blockchain? (Is decentralization necessary?)
- What type of blockchain is used? (Public, private, hybrid?)
- What consensus mechanism is employed? (Proof of Work, Proof of Stake, etc.)

Tip: Be cautious of projects that use blockchain as a buzzword without clearly justifying its role in the solution.

3. Examine the Technical Details

Key Components:

- Architecture: How does the blockchain work? Is it scalable and secure?
- Smart Contracts: Are there automated features for execution of transactions?
- Cryptography: What encryption methods are used for security?
- Transaction Throughput: Can the blockchain manage a high volume of transactions?

Tip: Technical complexity should be balanced with clarity. A good white paper explains the technology in terms both technical experts and non-experts can understand.

4. Assess Tokenomics

Key Questions:

- What is the role of the token in the ecosystem? (Utility, governance, or investment?)
- What is the total supply of tokens? Is it capped?
- How are tokens distributed? (E.g., to developers, investors, community incentives.)
- What mechanisms prevent inflation or manipulation of the token's value?

Tip: Be wary of projects with uneven token allocation or excessive control by founders.

5. Check the Roadmap

Key Questions:

- Does the roadmap clearly outline the project's goals and milestones?
- Are the timelines realistic?
- Has the team achieved past milestones, if applicable?

Tip: Projects with vague or overly aggressive roadmaps may lack feasibility.

6. Research the Team

Key Questions:

- Who are the core team members? What are their qualifications and experience?
- Are the advisors reputable and relevant to the project?
- Is the team transparent and accessible to the community?

Tip: Projects without a verifiable team or with anonymous founders may raise red flags.

7. Identify the Target Audience

Key Questions:

- Who is the project aimed at? (Businesses, developers, consumers?)
- Is the project addressing a niche or a broader market?
- Does the white paper explain how it will attract and retain users?

Tip: A well-defined target audience and market strategy indicate a thought-out project.

8. Look for Realistic Assumptions

Key Questions:

- Are the claims and promises realistic?
- Does the project provide clear metrics for success?
- Are there references or comparisons to similar projects?

Tip: Avoid projects that make exaggerated claims without evidence or data.

9. Analyze Security and Risk Mitigation

Key Questions:

- Does the white paper address potential risks?
- What measures are in place to ensure the security of the network and tokens?
- Is there a plan for regulatory compliance?

Tip: A strong white paper will acknowledge risks and outline strategies to overcome them.

10. Community and Ecosystem

Key Questions:

- How does the project plan to grow its user base?
- Are there partnerships with other companies or organizations?
- Is there a vibrant community supporting the project?

Tip: Projects with active communities and partnerships are more likely to succeed.

Red Flags to Watch For!

- Overly complicated language that lacks substance.
- Missing or vague technical details.
- Anonymous teams or unverifiable credentials.
- Unrealistic claims or aggressive timelines.
- Unbalanced token distributions that favor founders.

Analyzing a white paper requires a balance of technical understanding and critical thinking. By focusing on the vision, technology, tokenomics, team, and roadmap, you can make an informed decision about whether the project is worth your attention or investment.

Quiz: How to Analyze a Blockchain White Paper

Section 1: Understanding Vision

1. What is the primary purpose of a blockchain project's white paper?

a) To provide detailed information about the project's purpose, technology, and goals

b) To advertise the project to developers only

c) To guarantee success for investors

d) To replace traditional business plans

2. What should you look for in the project's vision?

a) A vague description of its purpose

b) Clear identification of the problem and how the blockchain addresses it

c) Promises of guaranteed returns on investment

d) A detailed explanation of unrelated blockchain technology

Section 2: Technology and Technical Details

3. Why is it important to assess the use of blockchain technology in a project?

a) To ensure that blockchain is necessary and not just used as a buzzword

b) To confirm the project's legality

c) To identify partnerships with government agencies

d) To determine if it is a private blockchain

4. What does scalability refer to in blockchain technology?

a) The ability of the blockchain to manage large volumes of transactions

b) The size of the blocks in the blockchain

c) The physical size of the blockchain's hardware

d) The number of users allowed to access the blockchain

5. Which aspect of blockchain security is most critical to evaluate in a white paper?

a) The use of smart contracts

b) The encryption method used for hashing data

c) The consensus mechanism and how it secures the network

d) The amount of investment raised during fundraising

Section 3: Tokenomics

6. What should you evaluate about a project's tokenomics?

a) The total supply of tokens and their distribution

b) How the tokens will be advertised on social media

c) Whether the tokens are physical or digital

d) The number of tokens allocated for legal compliance

7. Why is token distribution important?

a) It determines how the project will attract developers

b) It ensures fairness and prevents excessive control by founders

c) It guarantees the project's success

d) It limits the number of investors who can participate

Section 4: Roadmap and Team

8. What does a good roadmap include?

a) Vague goals and milestones

b) A timeline with clear, realistic goals and milestones

c) Only the launch date of the project

d) A list of future investors

9. Why is it important to research the team behind a blockchain project?

a) To confirm their qualifications and experience in relevant fields

b) To find out how much cryptocurrency they personally own

c) To ensure they are anonymous for privacy reasons

d) To verify that they have a social media presence

Section 5: Risks and Community

10. Why should a white paper address risks and risk mitigation?

a) To avoid any legal responsibility for the project

b) To show transparency and outline strategies to overcome challenges

c) To discourage potential investors from participating

d) To focus only on the advantages of the project

11. What is an indicator of a strong community around a blockchain project?

a) Active user engagement and partnerships with reputable organizations

b) A large number of followers on social media platforms

c) The absence of public discussions about the project

d) A small group of elite developers controlling the ecosystem

Answer Key
Section 1: Understanding Vision
a | 2. b
Section 2: Technology and Technical Details
3. a | 4. a | 5. c
Section 3: Tokenomics
6. a | 7. b
Section 4: Roadmap and Team
8. b | 9. a
Section 5: Risks and Community
10. b | 11. a

Conclusion

Blockchain and cryptocurrency are reshaping industries, economies, and societies. For teenagers, learning about these technologies fosters early financial literacy, critical thinking, and career readiness. For adults, it provides the tools to adapt to technological and economic shifts, ensuring they stay informed and competitive in the evolving world of 2025 and beyond.

Thank you for taking the time to explore these concepts through this book. I hope you find the writing educational, insightful, and inspiring as you continue to learn and engage with blockchain and cryptocurrency. If you find value in this book, I encourage you to share it with your family and friends, sparking conversations about the exciting possibilities of this transformative technology. Together, we can shape a more informed and empowered future.